SEA

AND PUGET SOUND

Michael's Co., Inc.

Photos on pages 1, 3, 5, 8, 9, 11 below, 15 above, 24 above, 26-27, 34-35 by Charles Adams, 36-37, 38 above, 41 below, 49, 50 above, 52 above, 56 above, 57, 58, 59, 62-63: courtesy of Michael's Co., Inc.

Printed in Italy by C.S.E.B. Sesto Fiorentino (Florence)

ISBN 2-84339-060-5

INTRODUCTION

The skyline of the largest city on the U.S. Northwest coast, Seattle, Washington.

Welcome to Seattle, the Emerald City! Situated in America's northwest state of Washington, this is the place that gave the world Starbucks Coffee, Boeing Aircraft, and Microsoft Computer Software. It also gave the world a more cerebral version of the laid-back west coast mindset than can be found to the south in sunny California. Maybe it is the cloudy and wet atmosphere that makes people more contemplative. Yet, Seattle's legendary rainfall is exaggerated. It only gets about thirty-six inches of precipitation each year - about the same amount that falls on Chicago. What makes it seem like more is that much of it comes in light mist-like showers, mainly between October and March. So while it might rain for hours on end, the total quantity that falls in the course of a day might not be enough to drown a flea. There is not much snowfall either because the temperature rarely dips below freezing. Summers, on the other hand, tend to be dry and warm, which is one reason why Seattle is a kind of outdoorsy haven. It is not just the nice summers that contribute to Seattle's recreational fame. Nature has blessed it with wonderful sporting opportunities. Its eastern edge fronts freshwater Lake Washington, and its western boundary lies along saltwater Puget Sound (which flows 125 miles north to the Strait of Juan de Fuca and to the Pacific Ocean beyond). With so much water, it is no wonder that Seattle is home to hundreds of thousands of watersport enthusiasts. Westward across Puget Sound lay the Olympic Mountains. (It is these mountains that cause most of the incoming rain from the Pacific Ocean to fall before it reaches Seattle.) Looking east in the other direction, the Cascade Mountains sit across from Lake Washington. They include the volcanoes of Mount Rainier, Glacier Peak, and what is left of Mount Saint Helens which riveted public attention when it blew its stack in 1980. Because of the nearby peaks, Seattle residents in search of a quick skiing fix or some other alpine adventure can fulfill their desires within a one-hour drive of the city.

Seattle is built on a series of hills, some of which rise five hundred feet above sea level and are quite steep. They provide some picture-perfect views of the bays, lakes, and mountains that surround the community. The city itself occupies eighty-four square miles of land, and is home to 550,000 people. Another 2.5 million live in the surrounding area. These people occupy one of the most liveable urban environments in the United States, with a mild climate, affordable housing, terrific sporting and cultural amenities, and good shops and restaurants.

Seattle is named after a famous Suquamish and Duwamish chief of the same name. In 1853, the early settlers baptized their community after him when their village was little more than an isolated but hopeful outpost on America's west coast frontier. These pioneers moved to Seattle to seek prosperity through exploiting the region's forest, fish, and other resources. As time passed, the growing population added industry to its entrepreneurial interests, of which one of the great successes was the Boeing aircraft company. It started out in 1918 during the days of wooden airplanes, utilizing the excellent supplies of timber to be had in the Northwest. Boeing expanded dramatically during World War II and now is the world's largest aircraft manufacturer. Its success is mirrored by newer Seattle-area companies, such as Starbucks and Microsoft, which dominate their respective fields throughout the world.

Often called the 'Gateway to the Orient' or the 'Gateway to Alaska,' Seattle's geographic location has helped the city prosper as a trade and transportation center. Because of the Panama Canal, it also ships huge quantities of goods to ports along the Gulf of Mexico and around the Atlantic Ocean.

The combination of a prosperous community, in a beautiful setting, with many attractions, makes Seattle an ideal destination for the traveler. With so much to see and do, the pages below offer an opportunity to sample some of the city's great attractions, explore its fascinating history, and partake in a taste of its cultural offerings.

A statue to Chief Seattle, after whom the city was named.
Opposite: upper: Mount Ranier looms in the distance; below: the city from Puget Sound.
Following pages: the lights of the evening skyline.

VANCE
HOTEL

SPACE NEEDLE

The most prominent building on the Seattle skyline is the Space Needle. Completed in 1961, it was the signature structure of the 1962 Seattle World's Fair. Known as the Century 21 Exposition, the fair's main theme was the promise of the future, including humanity's destiny in space. Today, the needle stands as a reminder of the fair and remains as one of the most popular attractions in the city.

The needle's design reflected the wide-eyed futurism of the early 1960s. Even the paint colors chosen for the building mirrored the cheerfulness of a more innocent time: 'Astronaut White' for the legs, 'Orbital Olive' for the center, 'Re-entry Red' for the halo, and 'Galaxy Gold' for the sunburst and roof.

The 605-foot needle is something of an engineering marvel. Because of its height and potential vulnerability to wind, it has a huge foundation, measuring thirty feet across and 120 deep. It took 467 cement trucks to fill that great hole. Thus anchored, the Space Needle can withstand winds of up to two hundred miles per hour. The great foundation also is meant to protect the Space Needle from earthquakes, as occurred in 1965 when a tremor measuring a nerve-wracking 6.5 on the Richter Scale struck.

Building the Space Needle and the other facilities of the 1962 World's Fair could not have come at a better time in the history of Seattle. The late 1950s was a bad time for the downtown because the inner city was dying. The fair helped reverse the downward spiral and heralded the beginning of a long period of florescence and enthusiasm in the life of the city. This change contributed significantly to making Seattle the urban success that it is today.

Seattle futuristic Space Needle, built for the 1962 World's Fair. Opposite: one of Washington's many ferries in the foreground, the majestic Cascade Mountains in the background.

While the 1962 World's Fair proved to be a great popular triumph, it also left the city with such amenities as the Science Center and a rebuilt Opera House. When Century 21 closed, the Space Needle and some of the other facilities became the nucleus of 'Seattle Center,' an urban park and cultural district developed between 1962 and 1964. Covering seventy-four acres of downtown land, Seattle Center is home to the architectural gems from 1962, plus fountains, landscaped open space, an amphitheater, indoor theaters, a stadium, a children's Fun Forest, convention facilities, and many restaurants and shops. Some businesses are housed in Center House, a fortress-like heritage building that once was an armory. Reinvigorated by the fair, people began to reshape the downtown. In 1964, the Seattle-First National Bank opened the first new building in the city to compete with the venerable Smith Tower of 1914 in height. Other projects followed during a period of enormous construction activity that continued through the years and which contributed to Seattle's dynamic and modern urban environment as well as to its impressive skyline.

Today the Space Needle offers a variety of things to see and do. The core attractions are the observation deck and its restaurants (one of which revolves). One of the other attractions that remains from the 1962 fair and that also is representative of the era's futurism is the Alweg Monorail. Originally it whisked fairgoers to Century 21. When new, the intention was to extend the monorail to the Seattle-Tacoma International Airport, but that never happened.

Perhaps the people of Seattle, like their fellow Americans, simply loved their cars too much to support the monorail, even if, as they were told, it was a harbinger of life in the twenty-first century. Today the monorail runs a distance of a little over a mile between Seattle Center and Westlake Mall.

Top: the Seattle skyline.
Bottom: a celebratory fireworks display at the Space Needle.

Two of Seattle Center's main attractions: the Pacific Science Center and the Space Needle.

PACIFIC SCIENCE CENTER

Located a short distance from the Space Needle, the Pacific Science Center is one of Seattle's landmark attractions. In striving to makes science fun and interesting, the center offers IMAX and laser theaters, a wide variety of exhibits - of which more than two hundred are interactive - and a diverse range of public programs. Among the permanent galleries, highlights include presentations on the human body, the world of dinosaurs, and the science of meteorology. Some exhibits include live creatures, such as the popular butterfly house and insect village. In addition, special galleries designed expressly for children help to make the center an excellent family destination.

WATERFRONT

Puget Sound defines the west face of Seattle. Yet, the city treated its waterfront badly through much of its history because it was used principally as a working port and industrial site. In recent decades, however, Seattle has reclaimed much of the waterfront as a public amenity, particularly between Piers 48 and 70.

Today, both tourists and locals flock to the waterfront where they eat and shop in the converted warehouses and other old port facilities, bask in the sun by the water's edge, pass their leisure hours in dockside cafes, watch boats sail by, or take in such local attractions as the Aquarium.

A stroll along the waterfront offers many opportunities to explore the diversity of the city's maritime life, whether it is to see the various ferries that sail from Seattle or to watch the city's famous fireboats (which often 'perform' for the public), or to visit the small Coast Guard Station and Museum (located a bit out of the main tourist area at Pier 36). One of the best ways to enjoying the waterfront is, of course, from the water. Several companies offer pleasant tours from different piers, and some host evening cruises where guests can listen to live music and gaze at the lights of the nighttime skyline.

The pleasures of the Seattle waterfront.
Following pages: skyscrapers hover over Elliott Bay, Seattle's large and deep harbor on Puget Sound.

PIER 56
ELLIOTT'S
RESTAURANT
SEATTLE'S CENTRAL WATERFRONT
OMNIDOME

ELLIOTT'S
"OYSTER HOUR"
MONDAY - FRIDAY
ARRIVES 3:30 PM
DEPARTS 6:30 PM
SPECIALLY PRICED SELECTED APPETIZERS
$1.00 OFF ALL DRAFT BEER
OYSTER & FERRY TRIVIA
OYSTER SHOTS
MEXICAN SHOT
PEPPER SHOT
LEMON SHOT
1.95
STOLY INFUSION
OYSTER DRAFTS
PYRAMID SEASONAL
RED HOOK SEASONAL ALE
PIKE PLACE ALE
2.50
EXIT

Crab Pot

ACRES OF CLAMS

56
Trident

THE
FISHERMANS
Restaurant & Bar

Visiting marine friends at the Seattle Marine Aquarium on Pier 59.
Opposite: in and about the ever popular waterfront.

SEATTLE MARINE AQUARIUM

Situated on Pier 59, the Seattle Marine Aquarium is a 'must see' attraction. Focused on the aquatic life of Puget Sound, visitors to the aquarium can enjoy innovative exhibits that recreate the underwater habitats of the sound's creatures and plant life. One of the highlights is the viewing dome where visitors can examine the different species of salmon and other fish that live near Seattle, along with such creatures as octopuses, barnacles, and shellfish, plus such kings of the food chain as sharks. Other popular creatures at the aquarium include sea otters and seals, who seem to devote their lives to eating and aquatic fooling around. Waterfowl also are on display outside at the site's own salt marsh. One of the interesting features of the Seattle Marine Aquarium is its fish ladder. It connects the aquarium's exhibits directly to Puget Sound and beyond to the open seas. Salmon fingerlings hatched at the aquarium swim away each year to pursue their lives in the Pacific. In the autumn, the now-grown fish return from the ocean, swim up the Sound, and jump back into the aquarium via the ladder.

Pike Place Market, a Seattle institution since 1907. The clock site is a favorite spot to gather on New Year's Eve.

PIKE PLACE OR PUBLIC MARKET CENTER

The Public (or Pike Place) Market is a Seattle institution dating back to 1907. Located off First Avenue between roughly Pike and Stewart streets, it occupies a site that was once underwater, but which has long since been filled in during the city's nineteenth- and early twentieth-century expansion. (The waterfront today lies a short distance farther west of the site.) Originally it was an open-air market, but the main building was erected in 1908. Within ten or so years other facilities were added.

When it started, the market was a place where city dwellers could buy rural produce directly from farmers at lower prices than they could from shopkeepers and other vendors. It quickly grew to include stalls selling fish and meats as well as farm produce from farther afield in California and elsewhere. As it became more popular, taverns, restaurants, bakeries, and other ventures opened, to be joined in more recent times by craftspeople, health food vendors, florists, antique dealers, and other retailers. The story of the market, nevertheless, was not always one of steady progress. Although it flourished in its early years, even doing well through much of the Great Depression, it was devastated in the 1940s when many Japanese-American farmers, fishers, and vendors were interned during the dark days of World War II. At the time, Euro-Americans feared sabotage and subversion from what in reality was fundamentally a loyal and law-abiding Asian population. After the return of peace, the market continued to limp along and its buildings deteriorated. Then, in the early 1960s, many people argued that it had become a blight on the landscape and ought to be torn down, to be replaced with office towers and parking garages. Concerned citizens, however, rallied to defend their market, and in 1971 the Pike Place Market became a designated historic district in an effort to save it from the wrecker's ball. The objective was to guarantee that the market would be preserved so that it could continue to have a life serving the people of the city.

Today, an enormous variety of businesses operate at the seven-acre, three-storey market which draws thousands of customers every day who want to find bargains, purchase specialty items, eat at one of its restaurants, or just savor the fair-like atmosphere of a busy and dynamic market where much fun is to be had spending one's money.

PUBLIC
MARKET
CENTER
MEET THE PRODUCE
FARMERS MARKET

18

An endless choice of fresh and delicious foods at the market.

A visit to the Pike Place Market presents a splendid introduction to the wide range of foodstuffs produced in Washington (along with an opportunity to buy the best that the rest of the world has to offer). The baked goods on sale regularly are made with wheat flour from the eastern end of the state where the weather is much drier and the soil is suitable for grain production. Washington also is famous for its fruit and vegetable crops, many of which are grown within fifty miles of Seattle, often on organic farms. With the Pacific Ocean located nearby, the market sells the freshest of fresh fish, with its salmon being justifiably renowned. Not to be forgotten by fish fanciers who patronize the market is the fact that Washington's lakes and rivers also boast an enormous variety of freshwater fish, such as trout, char, and whitefish, which are native to the state, as well as bass, perch, and catfish, which have been introduced to Washington's waters.

A bit of controversy looms over Pike Place Market today because it tries to serve two distinct audiences: tourists and locals. Out-of-towners patronize the craft shops, Seattle residents frequent the food stalls, but complain that there are too many tourists cluttering up the place. Despite the conflict, the market's tensions largely remain under the surface, so customers find much to enjoy, whether they are locals looking for dinner or are tourists in search of souvenirs. Furthermore, with its rich sights and smells, and its street musicians, everyone can enjoy the sheer excitement and bustle of this charming institution.

Above: the Seattle Art Museum.
Below and opposite: the Hammering Man and other works of outdoor art contribute to the pleasures of the Seattle environment.
Following pages: sleek office towers soar above the rough-and-ready tugboats of the working port.

SEATTLE ART MUSEUM

The Seattle Art Museum has two homes: its Asian wing located in Volunteer Park and the downtown Seattle Art Museum at 100 University Street. The latter site is the newer facility. It opened in 1991 in a building designed by award-winning architect Robert Venturi. Holding a collection of about 21,000 objects, the Seattle Art Museum is one of the most significant cultural institutions in the Northwest, exploring the art of a wide range of cultures, from ancient Egypt to contemporary America.

Seattle is home to a tremendous variety of artwork located out of doors as well as inside its museums and galleries. Perhaps the most famous is the *Hammering Man* at the Seattle Art Museum. Yet others can be seen throughout the city, where they enchant or puzzle passers-by and contribute to the ambiance of the urban landscape.

MUSEUM

SEATTLE·ART·MUSEUM

ZOBRIST MUSIC
GUITARS
LOANS

HERCULES

PIONEER SQUARE

Pioneer Square is Seattle's twenty-block downtown heritage district. It lies between Jackson and Cherry streets and Third Avenue and Alaskan Way. It is a good place to visit to gain a sense of the city's earlier history and take in some of the pleasures of the urban environment. Seattle's original settlers started out at Alki Point in 1851. However, they abandoned that site the next year for a more favorable location in the area of Pioneer Square. Seattle in those early years was very much a rugged frontier town, with alcohol abuse being the vice of choice. In those days, a sawmill cut lumber, and a skidway brought the logs to the mill along what today is Yesler Street. Back then, it was called Skid Road and gave birth to the euphemism 'Skid Row' for a down and out neighborhood. The community faced tragedy in 1889 when a fire broke out in a workshop. In the ensuing conflagration, most of the business district - constructed mainly out of wood - went up in flames. Nevertheless, the spirited people of Seattle quickly rebuilt their community, choosing this time to use brick rather than wood. The city's topography also changed radically during the late nineteenth and early twentieth centuries. Many hills were levelled or cut down to make for a flatter, more workable urban landscape. Some streets were raised as much as eighteen feet to level out the city, and the harbor was enlarged to meet the increasing needs of a growing and industrializing economy. Today, Pioneer Square is rich in book stores, antique shops, galleries, restaurants, and the other enterprises that help make life in an urban place civilized. It also boasts a number of little parks and outdoor attractions. One of Seattle's links to the far north is a reproduction of a Alaskan totem pole in a neighborhood park, erected to replace one lost to fire that had been put up in 1899. Another northern link is the Klondike Gold Rush National Historical Park on Main Street. It commemorates the great gold rush to Canada's Yukon Territory in the 1890s.

The people of Seattle played a leading role in hunting for gold and in supplying the adventurers who journeyed to the frozen northern wastelands. Seattle's mayor even resigned his office to pan for gold! In fact so many Americans traveled to the Yukon that the Canadian government sent troops to the territory in case all those Yankees decided to try to annex the goldfields to the United States!

The imposing Romanesque Revival Pioneer Building of 1889-91 dominates historic Pioneer Square.

UILDING
PIONEER S

STOP
ALL WAY

Above: visitors take in the sights from a relaxing horse-drawn carriage.
Below: Chief Seattle, the city's namesake.
Opposite: Smith Tower of 1910-14, once Seattle's tallest building.

SMITH TOWER

Constructed between 1910 and 1914, Smith Tower is one of the city's most famous landmarks. At forty-two stories, it not only was the tallest building in Seattle in its day, but was the fourth tallest structure in the world. (The other three were in New York.) It retained its standing as the city's highest building until the 1960s. At the time Smith Tower was erected, Seattle was a city of some 250,000 souls. The opening of the Panama Canal in 1914 dramatically increased Seattle's trade with the Atlantic world as it cut many thousands of miles off the sea journey to Europe and America's eastern seaboard. In the same year, the outbreak of World War I accelerated the demand for west coast produce and manufactured goods.

Smith Tower, because of is historical status and observation deck, has become something of a tourist attraction. Tourism is Washington State's fourth largest industry, and visitor dollars are a major contributor to Seattle's prosperity. For visitors, this means the city offers a wide range of good hotels and convention facilities to cater to their needs as it does its best to make all of these out-of-towners feel welcomed.

An enjoyable evening in Seattle.
Opposite: the caprice of a city's tenderloin district, both past and present.
Following pages: the cold light of day.

NIGHTLIFE IN SEATTLE

After the sun goes down, rock, jazz, classical, folk, grunge, and every other form of music anyone could possibly want to hear is offered in Seattle. Alternatively, there are coffee houses and bars where people can while away the evening hours in search of conversation or romance. And, of course, Seattle abounds in great restaurants, although, surprising, this is a relatively new phenomenon. Today, however, the city offers an immense range of culinary experiences, whether one wants to dine on fine food in the grand tradition, explore the varied cuisines of the world in the dozens of ethnic restaurants that dot the city, delight in the latest 'food fad,' or, of course, indulge in the magnificent bounty of the Pacific Ocean.

STATE
ROOMS 75¢
HOTEL

O.K. HOTEL
CAFE
LIVE ARTS · ENTERTAINMENT
CAFE

CAFE & CARDROOM
CAFE
CARDROOM
201

FIELD

WELCOME TO
SAFECO FIELD

DOWNTOWN

A glimpse at the downtown office towers tells any observer that Seattle must be a successful commercial center. But what is the basis of that success? Much of it lies in the import and export of goods, as it has since the earliest days of the community's life. Originally, the only way for people to send their produce to the outside world was by water. Rail service began in the 1880s and helped pump up the city's population from 3,500 in 1880 to 43,000 by 1890. Nevertheless, water transport always has remained pivotal. Today, Seattle receives goods from over forty nations and sends exports to over seventy countries. Cargoes shipped from Seattle's waterfront include wheat, flour, coal, lumber, rye, beans, oats, apples, and a massive range of high-tech and medical goods. In fact, international trade is the fastest growing sector in the economy of Washington State. Seattle's biggest industry is aviation, an enterprise dominated by the massive Boeing plant in the suburbs. Like many North American cities today, however, Seattle is becoming something of a 'post-industrial' community as new economic activities, service industries, retailing, tourism, and advanced technology either replace or supplement the endeavors of the past. One example of this change is shipbuilding. In the first half of the twentieth century, it was a huge enterprise in Seattle, focused on constructing ocean-going freighters and other vessels, but now it is limited to producing small fishing boats and pleasure craft. Forest industries of course continue to be important, but are not quite as critical to the city's prosperity as they once were. The same can be said for agriculture and fishing. Meanwhile computer industries have emerged as players of massive importance to the local economy because such important firms as Microsoft are based in the Seattle area.

Dusk falls over the busy city.

Good urban design and civic pride make for a congenial community.

Seattle's prosperity helps attract people from all over the world to work in its industries and enterprises. Once here, the city's beautiful Puget Sound setting, its sporting and outdoor opportunities, and its museums, nightlife, and restaurants, all influence these newcomers to stay put. To meet people's cultural interests, live theater presentations occur regularly, movie houses dot the city, and musical performances abound, whether it be some bar band at a local dive, a fine church choir celebrating the great music of the western tradition, professional music performed by the city's renowned symphony or opera company, a concert presented by a chamber ensemble, or an amateur production by one of a large number of community-based organizations. For particularly interesting performances, the people of Seattle know to check out the various dramatic and musical offerings at the University of Washington, which, like so many universities, greatly increases the cultural offerings and strength of its home community.

dryvit

Cafe
Santa Lucia

There are dozens of parks in Seattle and at least ten good beaches to add appeal to the urban setting, offering opportunities for both passive and energetic outdoor recreation. Many of the parks have special attractions in them, such as Seattle's famous zoo and pretty gardens in Woodland Park near Green Lake. In such a prosperous city as Seattle, golf naturally is popular, and the community's commitment to the democratic enjoyment of the outdoors is exemplified by the fact that it was the first place in the U.S. to open a public golf course, in Jefferson Park.
Fans of professional sports are well-served by Seattle teams housed in its excellent sports facilities. Baseball enthusiasts cheer on the Mariners during the long summer season, football fans root for the Seahawks, and basketball fanatics applaud the SuperSonics.
With all its amenities, quality of life, beautiful surroundings, and access to the great outdoors, it is no wonder that Seattle enjoys almost mythical status in the American mind as *the* place to live. *Money* magazine called it the 'Best Big Place to Live in the U.S.' while *Fortune* magazine has declared Seattle to be the 'Best City for Work and Family' - no small praise indeed at a time when many other cities worry about the viability of their downtowns and public amenities!

Urban scenes: the flavor of a deco sign, the ubiquitous American freeway, striking architecture, and an imposing convention center.

Broadway and its market: a place that caters to every taste in the Capitol Hill district.

BROADWAY

Like all great urban centers, Seattle's character is shaped in part by the different neighborhoods that form the city. One such district is the Capitol Hill area. Within it, Broadway is the main drag. Here one finds a trendy market between Republican and Harrison, with shops, services, and restaurants. Along Broadway itself, stores, restaurants, and bars cater to every taste. This is a part of the city that has seen some hard times but which now is experiencing its own renaissance. It also is a neighborhood of tremendous cultural, ethnic, and lifestyle diversity, and hence is representative of Seattle's life-and-let-live mentality. Diversity, however, was not always tolerated. Seattle's modern population is dominated by people of European ancestry, with the second largest group comprising people who trace their origins to Asia and the Pacific. Like the Europeans, they too have a long history in Seattle. Chinese settlers, for example, began to arrive in the 1860s. Sadly, they faced a considerable amount of discrimination and were the object of early race riots which forced many of them to leave. Nevertheless, some stayed, and their descendants represent almost 150 years of continuity in building the city into the tolerant place that it is today.

The wonderful Asian Art Museum in Volunteer Park, housed in a stunning 1933 building.

SEATTLE ASIAN ART MUSEUM

The original home of the Seattle Art Museum now is the site of the Seattle Asian Art Museum. The Art Moderne building which houses the Asian collection dates to 1933. It was built in large part through the efforts of a local doctor, Richard Fuller. Inspired by his mother, he generously founded the institution, utilizing his family's art collection as the nucleus of the museum's holdings. As the institution grew, the museum divided its collections between the old building in Volunteer Park and the new one on University Street. The old structure became the main site of its Asian holdings.

That collection is one of the best in the United States, with its assemblage of Japanese, Korean, and Chinese art being particularly noteworthy. The Seattle Asian Art Museum is one of a number of specialized institutions in Seattle that educate and entertain visitors and residents in search of cultural fulfillment. Others include the Museum of History and Industry, the Museum of Flight, the Henry Art Gallery, the Thomas Burke Memorial Washington State Museum, the Frye Art Museum, the Nordic Heritage Museum, the Wing Luke Memorial Museum of Chinese Culture, the Seattle Children's Museum, the Fort Lawton Military Museum, and the Postal Museum.

Volunteer Park's popular Conservatory of 1912.

CONSERVATORY

The City of Seattle constructed the Conservatory in 1912 in an effort to complete Volunteer Park according to designs of the sons of Frederick Law Olmstead, the famous American landscape architect of the nineteenth century. Originally called 'City Park' when created in 1878, it became 'Volunteer Park' in 1901 to honor soldiers who had served in the Spanish-American War of 1898 in which the United States entered the imperial expansion of the period by defeating Spain and picking up Puerto Rico, Guam, and the Philippines in the process.

The city developed the Conservatory's floral collection partly through generous donations from the public. In time, however, the Conservatory deteriorated and people worried that the building might have to be torn down. However, it was renovated between 1980 and 1985. Today, the Conservatory is divided into five 'houses.' Bromeliad, Fern, and Palm houses present a surprisingly interesting collection of tropical vegetation, including varieties of the pineapple plant, orchids, palms, and a great many other exotics. The temperate Seasonal Display House displays more common household plants as well as large floral displays that change with the weather. The arid Cactus House rounds out the Conservatory with a contrasting environment to the three tropical houses.

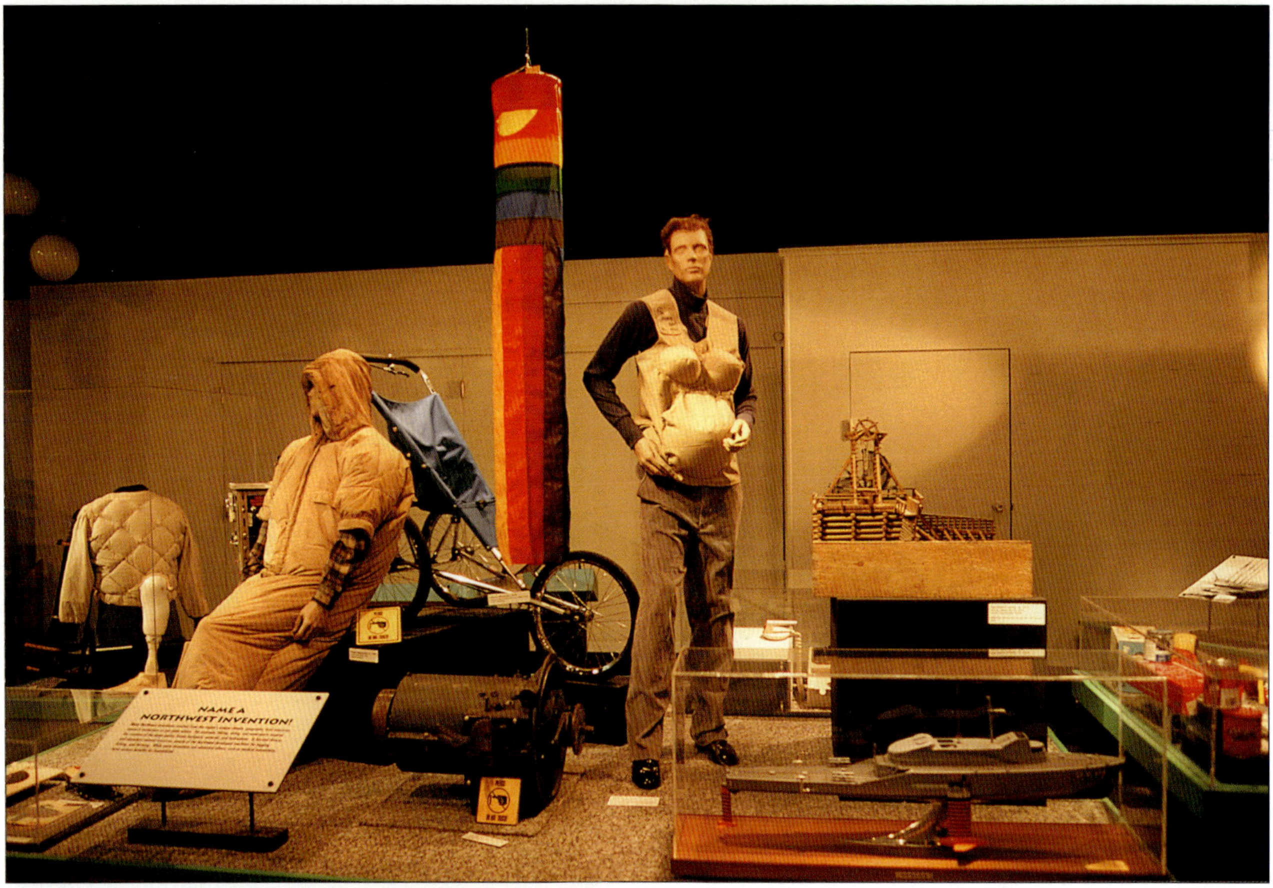

The Museum of History and Industry, the place to go for the lowdown on Seattle's past.

MUSEUM OF HISTORY AND INDUSTRY

The Museum of History and Industry on 24th Avenue East, near the Arboretum, is the place to go to investigate Seattle's interesting history. In both permanent and changing exhibits, artifacts, photographs, and dioramas present evocative surveys of Seattle's past from prehistoric days to modern times. One of the most popular exhibits is titled, 'Salmon Stakes: People, Nature, and Technology.' Using a mix of photographs, artifacts, and interactive devices, it explores how changing technologies have affected both the fish population and fishing industry workers over time in what traditionally has been one of the Northwest's major enterprises. Another favorite installation is 'The Great Seattle Fire of 1889' which examines this watershed event in the development of the city. It is complemented well by two other presentations. One is 'Seattle Roots' which invites visitors to examine the community's history from various viewpoints: rich and poor, young and old, and native, Asian, and Euro-American. As well, the 'Seattle in the 1880s' exhibit presents visitors with an opportunity to study the architecture of the late Victorian community. Beyond these thematic exhibits, the museum offers object-centered displays, such as its ever-popular collections of pleasure boat models and historical photographs.

CANADA
1976

The beautiful campus of the University of Washington.
Opposite: the cultured grace of the Japanese Garden at the Arboretum.

ARBORETUM AND JAPANESE GARDEN

One of Seattle's most beautiful places is the Arboretum in Washington Park. It attracts thousands of visitors each year to marvel at nature's beauty as presented within this magnificent preserve. Both regional and foreign plants are raised, so everyone who visits will be happy, whether local residents in search of the exotic, or tourists in search of the local. At the heart of the arboretum is the Japanese Garden, perhaps the most popular attraction of the site, especially during the spring blossom season when a riot of color and fragrance almost overwhelms the senses. Within this spectacular garden, the Japanese Tea House is a favorite destination, particularly when the traditional tea ceremony is performed. Near the garden is the Foster Island Nature Walk, a 1.5-mile trail along which people can watch boats in Lake Union and in the Chittenden (or Ballard) Locks. These locks are almost as large as those in the Panama Canal. Built between 1911 and 1916, they allow vessels to sail to and from Puget Sound. The walk also presents many opportunities for people to enjoy nature and relax, tour the small lock visitor center, and make their way to the trail's end at the popular Museum of History and Industry.

UNIVERSITY OF WASHINGTON

The University of Washington, located on the site of the 1909 Alaska-Yukon-Pacific Exposition, is Seattle's largest post-secondary institution, with a student body of about 35,000. It was founded in 1861, a remarkable achievement considering that Seattle at that time was not much more than a frontier town perched on the edge of the wilderness. The university occupies 640 pretty acres overlooking lakes Washington and Union, and offers some fine views of Mount Ranier and the Cascade Mountain Range. It boasts a massive sports stadium, a good medical school (where bone-marrow transplants were developed), and is regarded as one of the nation's better schools. As well, the university is noted for its attractive buildings, particularly the glorious Suzzallo Library of 1927, a kind of cathedral to the book.A visit to the university is particularly recommended during spring blossom time, and no trip would be complete without seeing the Henry Art Gallery and the Thomas Burke Memorial Washington State Museum housed on the campus. The former exhibits a nice collection of European and American art from the nineteenth and twentieth centuries. The latter is famous for its outstanding collection of west coast and Alaskan aboriginal artifacts as well as its natural history displays.

The bustling Fisherman's Terminal with its notable Fisherman's Memorial at Salmon Bay.

FISHERMAN'S TERMINAL

The home port for the U.S. North Pacific fishing fleet is Fisherman's Terminal, located on the channel between Puget Sound and Lake Union. This is very much a working waterfront area, and therefore offers a chance to experience the unvarnished side of Seattle life that tourists often miss. The fleet that ties up at the terminal travels far and wide in search of salmon and such other species as herring, halibut, smelt, and anchovies. Fisherman's Terminal serves as a reminder of how vital marine industries have been to Seattle. In the first half of the twentieth century, for instance, the city experienced shipbuiding booms, particularly during the two world wars. The expansion of marine construction during the early 1900s - when strife between industrial barons and their labor forces was common - saw the first general strike in American history take place in Seattle in 1919 when efforts were made to lower wages at the yards. This sort of tension continues today as the fishers of the terminal worry about their future in the face of depleting fish stocks and competition from the Canadian and other fleets on the Pacific Ocean.

WILD SALMON
SEAFOOD ◆ MARKET

Above: the Museum of Flight.
Below and opposite: the Boeing Plant in the world's largest building.

MUSEUM OF FLIGHT AND BOEING INDUSTRIES

The Museum of Flight, located at 9404 East Marginal Way, presents a terrific collection of aircraft and aviation nostalgia. It is the largest such institution on the west coast, and explores the history of flight from its earliest days to the space age, with a particular focus on the aviation history of the Pacific Rim.

The Great Gallery is the highlight of the site because a large number of famous aircraft are on display. Among them is a celebrated B-17 'Flying Fortress' bomber of the Second World War, the first presidential jet, the world's only existing MD-21 Blackbird spy plane and drone, and a rare World War II FG-1D Corsair rescued from Lake Washington.

To meet people's interests beyond the static displays of the Museum of Flight, numerous airshows take place in the Seattle area throughout the year, including breathtaking formation flying by modern military aircraft as well as nostalgic flypasts by some of the famous airplanes of earlier eras. And of course, all this interest in skyward things means that skydiving and ballooning are popular pursuits for both participants and spectators in the Seattle region.

Boeing helps to meet people's interests in aircraft heritage and aviation with tours of its magnificent Everett factory north of Seattle. There, the company showcases its aircraft production lines in a truly awe-inspiring location because the Boeing factory is the biggest building in the world (at 472 million cubic feet). Boeing builds its famous aircraft for many of the world's airlines, so the plant is always busy, and planes in various states of assembly usually can be seen. Hence, this is a fascinating destination for visitors and an excellent complement to the historical focus of the Museum of Flight.

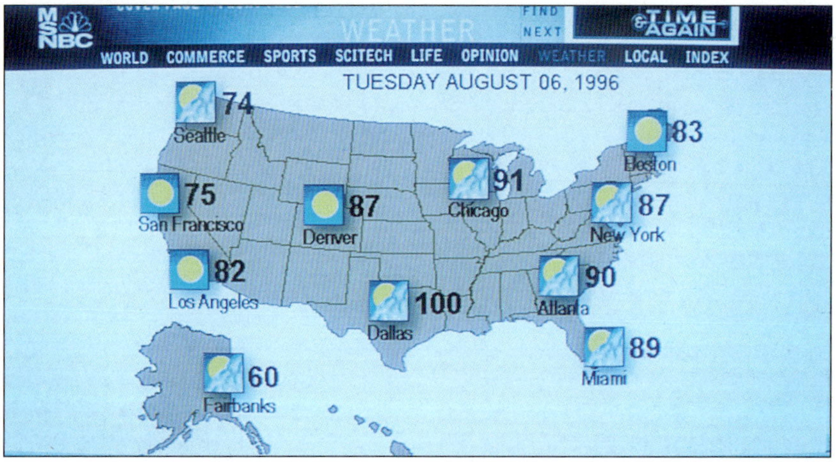

Inside Microsoft's corporate museum in Redmond, a Seattle suburb.

MICROSOFT MUSEUM

Microsoft, the most talked-about corporation in the world these days, is headquartered in the suburban community of Redmond, east of Seattle. With thousands of workers on its huge campus, Microsoft naturally is home to a number of amenities for its employees and their families. One of them is Microsoft's corporate museum, which tells the company's story through both traditional exhibits and, naturally, with some quite dynamic interactive computer technology. With over two thousand computer firms in the region, locating a computer museum in the Seattle area makes a lot of sense!

Redmond is just one of many places near Seattle that draws visitors. Others include the spectacular Snoqualmie Falls east of the city, and, of course, the ever-magnificent Cascade and Olympic mountains.

PLE, OUR MOST IMPORTA
COULD
THAT
BE TRUE?
United Way
A GOOD CORPORATE CITIZE
THE MICROSOFT WAY
VIDEO

Olympic Games
Ostler, Albom take unique look at medals
Dole unveils plan to cut taxes
MSNB

COULD
THAT
E TRUE?
Touching someone's life
A show of support

The Alki Point Lighthouse stands on a site where the first light began to guide vessels to Seattle in 1881. Meanwhile, pleasure seekers enjoy the beach or head for their boats.

ALKI BEACH

Alki Beach, located in West Seattle, south of Elliott Bay, is the site where the first pioneers arrived in the area in 1851. These people - five families from Illinois - immediately started to cut timber to supply a building boom in San Francisco. They deserted the site in 1852 because of high winds and a poor anchorage in order to relocate to a better site near Elliott Bay around today's Pioneer Square. Abandoned, the Alki area developed slowly, but began to grow late in the nineteenth century when a ferry service started to run between it and the city. A trolley car replaced the ferry in 1902 which accelerated growth. Seattle annexed the area in 1907.
A year later, the city began to develop Alki Beach as a public amenity, combining natural environments, a wonderful beach, and other attractions.
Today, people descend on the area's 2.5 miles of beaches to swim (in what admittedly is some pretty cold water), soak up the sun, walk along the promenade, watch passing boats, do some birdwatching, and otherwise occupy their time in self-indulgent relaxation and recreation, often with a view towards kindling a romance.

A lift bridge at the Hiram M. Chittenden locks.
Opposite: above: one of the city's floating bridges heading out of town; below: a more picturesque escape by ferry.

SEATTLE'S FLOATING BRIDGES

With so much water surrounding Seattle, it is no wonder that the city is served by an impressive fleet of ferry boats and an unusual assortment of bridges, the most interesting being the 'floating bridges.' One of them is the 1.25-mile Lake Washington (or Lacey V. Murrow) Floating Bridge, originally completed in 1939 to replace ferry service between the city and Mercer Island. It was built on twenty-five floating concrete sections anchored to the bottom of the lake. Each of them is 350 feet long, fifty-nine wide, and fourteen high, and is linked to the others by cables. Each section contains ninety-six watertight cells. These cells are filled or emptied of water on a seasonal basis so that the bridge can be raised or lowered with the annual change in the lake's water level. The bridge itself rests on top of these sections and is perfectly capable of withstanding ninety-mile-per-hour winds and six-foot waves. (Nevertheless, the current one is a replacement - the original sank in 1990!) The other noted floating bridge (the world's longest at 1.4 miles), also is on Lake Washington. It is the Evergreen Point Floating Bridge which connects Seattle to Bellevue and Kirkland. The reason why floating bridge technology is used is that Lake Washington cannot be crossed utilizing traditional bridge-building techniques. It is too deep at two hundred feet, and the bottom is too soft and unstable to support the piers of a conventional bridge. As well as the floating bridges, Seattle is home to six drawbridges which open tens of thousands of times each year to let vessels sail past them. All these bridges, however, do not obviate the need for ferry service. So, Washington State Ferries, largely centered in Seattle, boast the nation's most extensive automobile ferry system and connect the city with the Olympic Peninsula, several islands in Puget Sound, and the Canadian city of Victoria, on Vancouver Island to the north.

These bridges, the road network, and ferries all provide quick and easy access to the attractions that lie just outside of Seattle, such as some of the finest hiking, climbing, fishing, and skiing opportunities on the west coast - and that is saying something! One popular destination among tourists is Blake Island in Puget Sound, accessible by tour boat. This large island attracts visitors with its Tillicum Village, a place where traditional native-style salmon is served and where aboriginal performers present the dances of the different tribes of the Pacific Coast.

Chief Seattle's tomb, across Puget Sound from his namesake city. Following pages: snow-capped Mount Ranier sits majestically to the east of Seattle.

SEATTLE TOMB

The city is named after the famous native leader, Chief Seattle. Born around 1786 on an island in Puget Sound to a noble family among the Suquamish and Duwamish peoples, he entered the world during a period of deep crisis among the aboriginal nations of the Northwest. At that time, Euro-American influences had begun to be felt as trade goods entered tribal society and as foreign diseases decimated an indigenous population that had no natural immunities to the contagions introduced by the newcomers.

Seattle was baptized by Roman Catholic missionaries in 1847, who renamed him Noah because of his interest in the Biblical story of the Flood, which resonated well with Suquamish flood mythology. About the same time, he gave up the way of the warrior and chose to work as a diplomatic leader. When Americans began to settle the Washington area in earnest, they chose to deal with Seattle as the leader of the regional native groups. He befriended the newcomers, and they in turn honored him by naming the new settlement on Puget Sound after him in 1853.

The native society into which Chief Seattle had been born was an ancient one. People had begun to inhabit the Northwest coast of North America sometime between six- and twelve thousand years ago. At first, they settled along the many rivers that flow into the Pacific, but later they gradually expanded along the coast and islands and drew most of their subsistence from the salt water world. As time passed, the different cultural groups developed prosperous and sophisticated societies that were marked, in part, by their exquisite artistry that is appreciated so much today.

Europeans began to penetrate North America's Pacific coast in the eighteenth century. Russians came first, in the 1740s, then the Spanish and the British (including Captain James Cook) explored the region in the 1770s. In subsequent years the local indigenous people traded furs and other goods for metal tools, cloth, luxury items, and other wares. While the new goods made some aspects of aboriginal life easier, this period also heralded the beginning of decades of social disintegration, population loss, mistreatment by settlers, and other crises. It was Chief Seattle's unenviable task to protect his people's interests during this time of rapid and unhappy change, a task he fulfilled to the best of his abilities until his death in 1866.